WeeSing® & Learn
COLORS

Library of Congress Catalog Number: 00-132217
ISBN 0-8431-0226-8   A B C D E F G H I J

Wee Sing® & Learn
COLORS

by Pamela Conn Beall and Susan Hagen Nipp
illustrated by Yudthana Pongmee

PSS!
PRICE STERN SLOAN

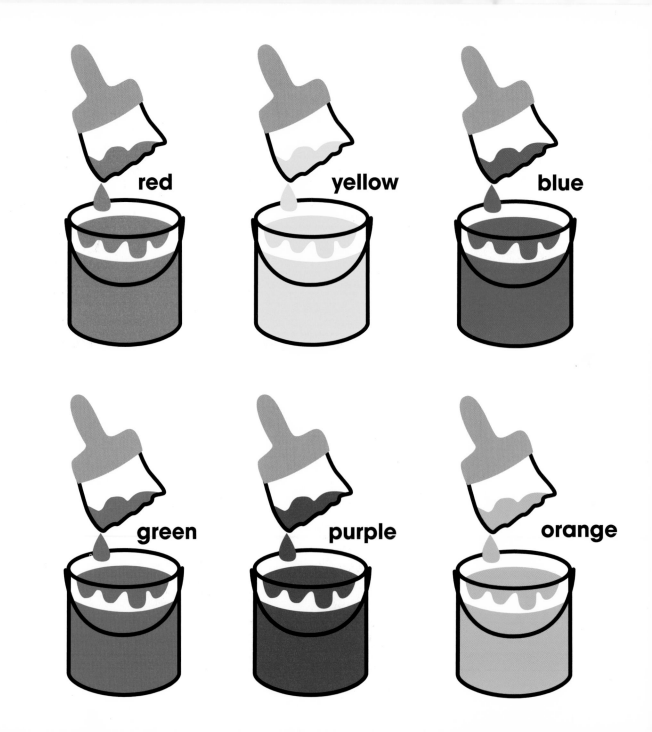

red

yellow

blue

green

purple

orange

pink

brown

black

gray

white

red

red wagon

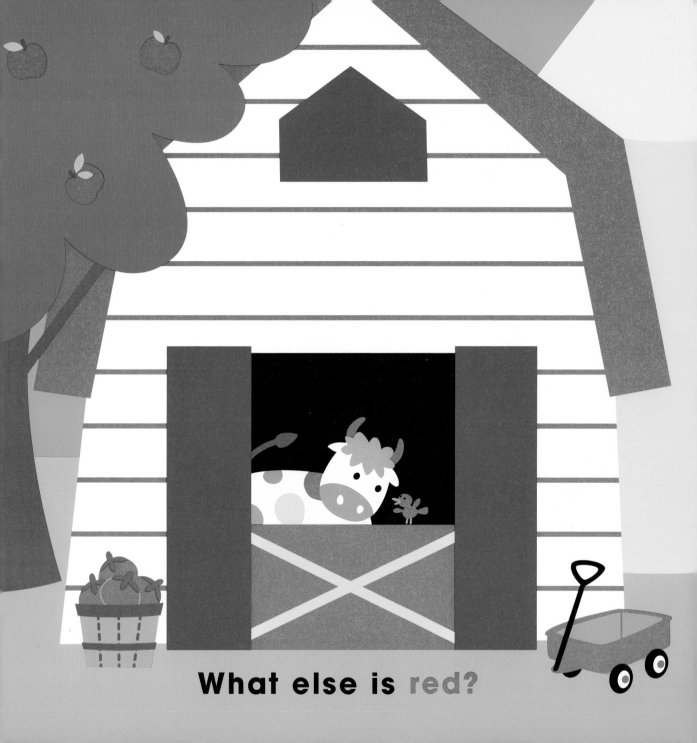

What else is red?

yellow

yellow sun

What else is yellow?

blue

bluebird

What else is blue?

green

green frog

What else is green?

purple

purple plum

What else is purple?

orange

orange pumpkins

What else is orange?

pink

pink piggies

What else is pink?

brown

brown horse

What else is brown?

black

black hen

What else is black?

gray

gray squirrel

What else is gray?

white

white lamb

What else is white?

Find all the colors on the farm.

Mixing colors...

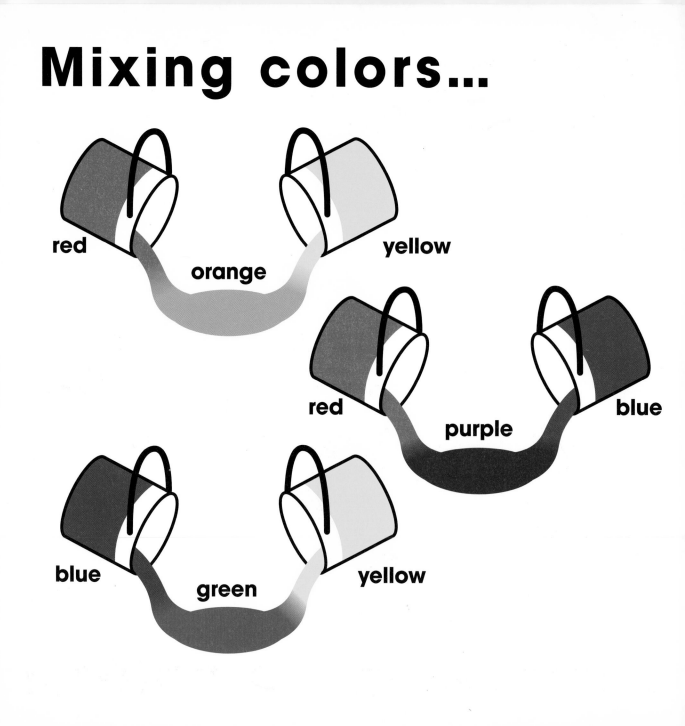

red

yellow

orange

red

purple

blue

blue

green

yellow

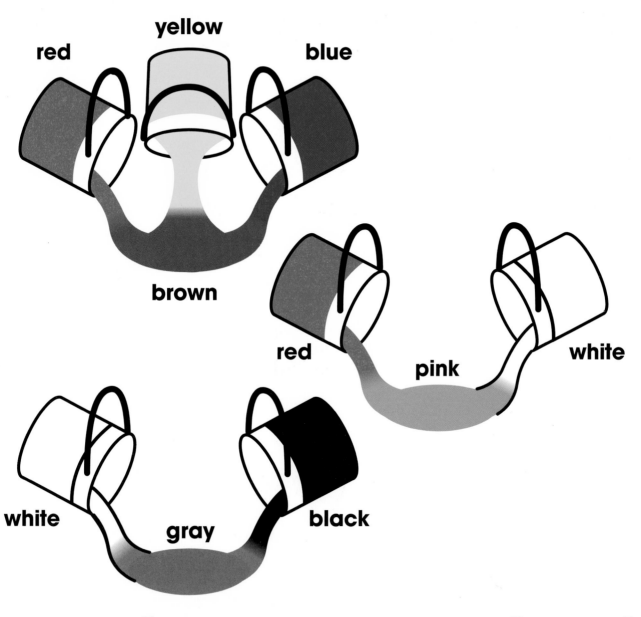

red yellow blue

brown

red pink white

white gray black

...makes more colors!